At Play in the Community

M000238823

Contents

Judy Nayer

Everyone Plays

Let's play!
Let's paint. Let's jump.
Let's splash. Let's sway.

Everyone needs to play.

Places to Play

Go for a run at a **public** park, hike up a mountain, or play ball on a court.

Every **community** has places to play.

You can learn and play at a science center. Grown-ups who work there will help you have fun!

Sometimes, your family and neighbors join in when you play. An uncle can be an umpire. A store can **sponsor** a team.

Some of the places where you can play are **businesses**. People pay to play there. Who might help you play at these businesses?

Playing and Helping

We all like to play just for fun, but you can play to help others, too!

Running can help raise money for people who are sick.

How can reading a book help?

A garden can make a community more beautiful. How are these people helping?

Who Helps Us Play?

Our **government** helps us play. We pay the government money called **taxes**.

Our government uses some of the tax money to pay for places, workers, and **equipment** for play.

Your **neighborhood** may want to close off a street for a block party.

Work Sheet Requesting a Block Party

Name of Event: Summer Block Party

Event Date: July 4, 2003

Request is Being Made by and/or Co-sponsored by: (mark accordingly)

☐ School   ☒ Neighborhood Association   ☐ Business

☐ City Government   ☐ State Government

Reason for Event: Fourth of July Celebration

Location: Elmwood Street

Answer Information Question: (insert Y = yes, N = no)   Answer

1. Is this event for fund-raising purposes?   N
2. Is this event open to the public?   N
3. Is this event using all volunteer workers?   Y
4. Will there be entertainment on the street?   Y
5. Will food be served or consumed on the street?   Y

Name of Organization: Elmwood Neighborhood Assoc.

Telephone number: 260-555-5555   **Fax Number:**

Name of Person in Charge:

Telephone number: **Fax Number:**

Authorized Signature: **Date:**

First, you must ask your town or city government for permission.

How do you think the community is helping these people play?